CARYL CHURCHILL

Caryl Churchill has written for the stage, television and radio. Her stage plays include *Owners* (Royal Court Theatre Upstairs, 1972); *Objections to Sex and Violence* (Royal Court, 1975); *Light Shining in Buckinghamshire* (Joint Stock on tour, incl. Theatre Upstairs, 1976); *Vinegar Tom* (Monstrous Regiment on tour, incl. Half Moon and ICA, 1976); *Traps* (Theatre Upstairs, 1977), *Cloud Nine* (Joint Stock on tour, incl. Royal Court, London, 1979, then Theatre de Lys, New York, 1981); *Three More Sleepless Nights* (Soho Poly and Theatre Upstairs, 1980); *Top Girls* (Royal Court, London, then Public Theatre, New York, 1982); *Fen* (Joint Stock on tour, incl. Almeida and Royal Court, London, then Public Theatre, New York, 1983); *Softcops* (RSC at the Pit, 1984); *A Mouthful of Birds*, with David Lan (Joint Stock on tour, incl. Royal Court, 1986); *Serious Money* (Royal Court and Wyndham's, London, then Public Theatre, New York, 1987); *Icecream* (Royal Court, London, 1989); *Mad Forest* (Central School of Speech and Drama, then Royal Court, London, 1990, then New York Theatre Workshop, 1991); *Lives of the Great Poisoners* (with Orlando Gough and Ian Spink, Second Stride on tour, incl. Riverside Studios, London, 1991); *The Skriker* (Royal National Theatre, London, 1994; Public Theatre, New York, 1996); and *Thyestes*, translated from Seneca (Royal Court Theatre Upstairs, London, 1994).

by the same author

Caryl Churchill

LIGHT SHINING IN BUCKINGHAMSHIRE

NICK HERN BOOKS
London

A Nick Hern Book

This edition of *Light Shining in Buckinghamshire* first published in 1989 by Nick Hern Books. New edition published in 1996 by Nick Hern Books, 14 Larden Road, London W3 7ST

Reprinted 1999, 2000, 2002

Light Shining in Buckinghamshire first published in Great Britain in 1978 by Pluto Press Ltd. Published in Methuen's World Dramatists anthology edition 1985

Set in Baskerville by Book Ens, Saffron Walden, Essex
Printed and bound by Cox & Wyman Ltd, Reading, Berkshire

ISBN 1 85459 311 0

A CIP catalogue record for this book is available from the British Library

Caryl Churchill

A Chronology of Performed Plays

PLAY	WRITTEN	PERFORMED (s=stage, r=radio, t=television)
Downstairs	1958	1958s
You've No Need to be Frightened	1959?	1961r
Having a Wonderful Time	1959	1960s
Easy Death	1960	1961s
The Ants	1961	1962r
Lovesick	1965	1966r
Identical Twins	?	1968r
Abortive	1968?	1971r
Not . . . not . . . not . . . not . . . not enough oxygen	?	1971r
Schreber's Nervous Illness	?	1972r
Henry's Past	1971	1972r
The Judge's Wife	1971?	1972t
Owners	1972	1972s
Moving Clocks Go Slow	1973	1975s
Turkish Delight	1973	1974t
Perfect Happiness	1973	1973r
Objections to Sex and Violence	1974	1975s
Traps	1976	1977s
Vinegar Tom	1976	1976s
Light Shining in Buckinghamshire	1976	1976s
Floorshow (contributor to)	1977	1977s
The After Dinner Joke	1977	1978t
The Legion Hall Bombing	1978	1979t
Softcops	1978	1983s
Cloud Nine	1978	1979s

Three More Sleepless Nights	1979	1980s
Crimes	1981	1981t
Top Girls	1980–2	1982s
Fen	1982	1983s
A Mouthful of Birds (with David Lan)	1986	1986s
Serious Money	1987	1987s
Icecream	1988–9	1989s

Light Shining in Buckinghamshire

You great Curmudgeons, you hang a man for stealing,
when you yourselves have stolen from your brethren all
land and creatures.

More Light Shining in Buckinghamshire, a Digger pamphlet
1649

A revolutionary belief in the millenium went through the
middle ages and broke out strongly in England at the time
of the civil war. Soldiers fought the king in the belief that
Christ would come and establish heaven on earth. What
was established instead was an authoritarian parliament,
the massacre of the Irish, the development of capitalism.

For a short time when the king had been defeated
anything seemed possible, and the play shows the amazed
excitement of people taking hold of their own lives, and
their gradual betrayal as those who led them realised that
freedom could not be had without property being
destroyed. At the Putney Debates Cromwell and Ireton
argued for property; Gerrard Winstanley led Diggers to take
over the common land: 'There can be no universal liberty
till this universal community be established.' The Levellers
and Diggers were crushed by the Army, and many turned
in desperation to the remaining belief in the millenium,
that Christ would come to do what they had failed in. The
last long scene of the play is a meeting of Ranters, whose
ecstatic and anarchic belief in economic and sexual
freedom was the last desperate burst of revolutionary
feeling before the restoration.

The simple 'Cavaliers and Roundheads' history taught at
school hides the complexity of the aims and conflicts of
those to the left of Parliament. We are told of a step
forward to today's democracy but not of a revolution that
didn't happen; we are told of Charles and Cromwell but
not of the thousands of men and women who tried to
change their lives. Though nobody now expects Christ to
make heaven on earth, their voices are surprisingly close to
us.

C.C. 1978

A Note on the Production

The characters Claxton and Cobbe are loosely based on Laurence Clarkson, or Claxton, and Abiezer Coppe, or Cobbe, two Ranters whose writings have survived; the others are fictional, except for those in the Putney Debates, which is a much-condensed transcript of three days of debate among Army officers and soldiers' delegates which took place in 1647.

The characters are not played by the same actors each time they appear. The audience should not have to worry exactly which character they are seeing. Each scene can be taken as a separate event rather than part of a story. This seems to reflect better the reality of large events like war and revolution where many people share the same kind of experience. I recommend other productions to distribute parts in the same way, since the play was constructed with this in mind; and there would be difficulties if each character was played by one actor – for instance, Brigg's friend in the recruiting scene is by implication Claxton, from the reference to the baby, yet in the last scene Briggs and Claxton meet as strangers. When different actors play the parts what comes over is a large event involving many people, whose characters resonate in a way they wouldn't if they were more clearly defined.

The play was performed with a table and six chairs, which were used as needed in each scene. When any chairs were not used they were put on either side of the stage, and actors who were not in a scene sat at the side and watched the action. They moved the furniture themselves. Props were carefully chosen and minimal.

Scenes:	Parts played by:
COBBE PRAYS	Nigel
THE VICAR TALKS TO HIS SERVANT	Colin and Bob
MARGARET BROTHERTON IS TRIED	Janet, Colin and Will
STAR RECRUITS	Bob as Star, Will as Briggs, Colin as Friend, and the rest
BROTHERTON MEETS THE MAN	Janet and Bob
BRIGGS JOINS UP	Nigel as Briggs, Bob as Star
HOSKINS INTERRUPTS THE PREACHER	Nigel, Linda, and the rest
CLAXTON BRINGS HOSKINS HOME	Linda as Wife, Janet as Hoskins, Will
COBBE'S VISION	Bob announcing, Colin as Cobbe
TWO WOMEN LOOK IN A MIRROR	Janet and Linda
BRIGGS RECALLS A BATTLE	Nigel
THE PUTNEY DEBATES	Nigel as Rainborough, Bob as Sexby, Linda as Rich, Janet as Wildman, Colin as Cromwell, Will as Ireton

DIGGERS	All
CLAXTON EXPLAINS	Will
BRIGGS WRITES A LETTER	Bob and Colin
THE WAR IN IRELAND	Colin
THE VICAR WELCOMES THE NEW LANDLORD	Will and Nigel
A WOMAN LEAVES HER BABY	Linda and Janet
A BUTCHER TALKS TO HIS CUSTOMERS	Bob
LOCKYER'S FUNERAL	Nigel
THE MEETING	Janet as Hoskins, Linda as Brotherton, Colin as Cobbe, Will as Claxton, Nigel as Briggs, Bob as the Drunk
AFTER	Same as the meeting

Documentary material:

Fear, and the pit . . . Isaiah 24, xvii–xx
A Fiery Flying Roll Abiezer Coppe 1649
All Seems Beautiful . . . *Song of Myself* Walt Whitman
The Putney Debates 1647
The True Levellers Standard Advanced Gerrard Winstanley, 1649
The English Soldier's Standard to Repair to 1649
The Moderate, a Leveller newspaper, 1649
The sleep of the labouring man . . . Ecclesiastes 5

List of characters in order of appearance:

COBBE, a gentleman
VICAR, an Anglican
SERVANT
1ST JP
2ND JP
MARGARET BROTHERTON, a vagrant
STAR, a corn merchant
BRIGGS, a working man
FRIEND, a working man
MAN, a vagrant
PREACHER, a Calvinist
HOSKINS, a vagrant preacher
CLAXTON, a working man
CLAXTON'S WIFE
1ST WOMAN
2ND WOMAN
COLONEL THOMAS RAINBOROUGH, a Leveller, from
Cromwell's army
EDWARD SEXBY, an elected representative from
Cromwell's army
COLONEL NATHANIEL RICH
JOHN WILDMAN, a gentleman
OLIVER CROMWELL
GENERAL IRETON
WINSTANLEY
BUTCHER
DRUNK, a poor man

Light Shining in Buckinghamshire opened at the Traverse Theatre, Edinburgh, in September 1976, and was then on tour and at the Royal Court Theatre Upstairs.

Actors in the workshop:
Ian Charleson
Jenny Cryst
Linda Goddard
Carole Hayman
Will Knightley
Colin McCormack
Anne Raitt
David Rintoul

Actors in the play:
Janet Chappell
Linda Goddard
Bob Hamilton
Will Knightley
Colin McCormack
Nigel Terry

When Janet Chappell had to leave the cast her parts were played by Carole Hayman.

Directed by Max Stafford-Clark
Designed by Sue Plummer
Lighting by Steve Whitson
Music by Colin Sell

LIGHT SHINING IN BUCKINGHAMSHIRE

ACT ONE

ALL (*sing Isaiah 24 xvii–xx*).

Fear, and the pit, and the snare are upon thee,
O ·inhabitant of the earth.
And it shall come to pass that he who fleeth
from the noise of the fear shall fall into the
pit; and he that cometh out of the midst of the
pit shall be taken in the snare; for the windows
from on high are open, and the foundations of
the earth do shake.
The earth is utterly broken down, the earth
is clean dissolved, the earth is moved
exceedingly.
The earth shall reel to and fro like a drunkard,
and shall be removed like a cottage; and the
transgression thereof shall be heavy upon it;
and it shall fall and not rise again.

COBBE PRAYS

COBBE. Forgive my sins of the night and already this
new day. Oh prevent me today from all the
sins I will note – action, word, thought or faint
motion less than any of these – or commit
unknowing despite my strict guard set. Sloth
not rising when mother called, the air so cold,
lay five minutes of sin till she called again.
Break me, God, to welcome your cold. Lust
when the girl gave meat last night, not keeping
my eyes on my plate but followed her hand.
Repented last night with groans to you, O
God, and still dreamt. Guard me today. Let
me not go to hell, hot nor cold hell, let me be
one of your elect. What is worst, I am not
praying to you about the worst sin. I sin in my
fear of praying about that sin, I sin in denying
my fear. But you cut through that mesh,

knowing. Why is it not enough to use your
name in prayer, oh God, oh Lord Jesus Christ,
amen, this is prayer, oh God, no swearing.
Rich men of Antichrist on horses swear, king's
officers say 'dammee' laughing. The beggar
swore when they whipped him through the
street and my heart leapt at each curse, a curse
for each lash. Is he damned? Would I be? At
table last night when father said grace I
wanted to seize the table and turn it over so
the white cloth slid, silver, glass, capon, claret,
comfits overturned. I wanted to shout your
name and damn my family and myself eating
so quietly when what is going on outside our
gate? Words come out of my mouth like toads,
I swear toads, toads will sit on me in hell. And
what light on my father, still no light? Not to
honour my father is sin, and sin to honour a
greedy, cruel, hypocritical – Is it sin to kneel
here till he leave the house? I cannot go down
to him. It is sin to go down. I will wait till I
hear the door. To avoid his blessing.

THE VICAR TALKS TO HIS SERVANT (CLAXTON)

The VICAR *sits at table, with wine and oranges.*

VICAR.   How's the baby today? Any better?

SERVANT.   No, sir.

VICAR.   You saw who were missing again from
            morning service.

SERVANT.   Sir.

VICAR.   No better – no worse, I hope?

SERVANT.   Yes, sir.

VICAR.   Good, good. The sermon would have done
            them good. It wasn't my own, you could
            probably tell. The Bishop's naturally more
            gifted. But it's no good having it read in every
            parish if nobody compels the tenants to hear

it. It's the ones who weren't there that I was talking to. 'From whence come wars and fightings among you?' From their lusts, from greed and envy and pride, which are from the devil, that's where the wars come from. When you said yes, you meant no worse?

SERVANT. No sir.

VICAR. Worse.

SERVANT. Sir.

VICAR. God tries you severely in your children. It must have been a comfort this morning to have the Bishop himself encourage you to suffer. 'Be afflicted and mourn and weep.' That is the way to heaven.

SERVANT. Sir.

He pours more wine.

VICAR. Why we have this war is because men want heaven now. If God meant us to have heaven on earth, why did he throw us out of paradise? They're fighting God himself, do they know that? They must be brought before the magistrates and forced to come next Sunday, and I'll tell them in my own words. Thank you, a little. This is a godly estate and they will be evicted if they don't submit.

He gives SERVANT an orange.

Still we must pray your baby is spared this time. Take it an orange.

He drinks and takes an orange.

SERVANT. Thank you, sir.

VICAR. And if it is not spared, we must submit. We all have to suffer in this life.

He drinks.

MARGARET BROTHERTON IS TRIED

She is barely audible.

1ST JP.   Is this the last?

2ND JP.   One more.

1ST JP.   It's a long list.

2ND JP.   Hard times.

1ST JP.   Soft hearts. Yours.

2ND JP.   Step forward please.

1ST JP.   I still say he should have been hanged.

2ND JP.   He'll die in jail. Name?

BROTHERTON. Margaret Brotherton.

1ST JP.   That's no example, nobody sees it.

2ND JP.   Margaret Brotherton. Begging. Guilty or not guilty?

BROTHERTON. I don't know what you mean . . .

1ST JP.   You're not of this parish?

2ND JP.   Where do you come from?

BROTHERTON. Last week I was at Aston Clinton, and before that from Northampton.

1ST JP.   I don't want to be told every place you've ever been. Where were you born?

BROTHERTON. Long Buckby.

1ST JP.   If you belong fifty miles away what are you doing here?

2ND JP.   Have you relations here? Friends you could stay with?

1ST JP.   Tell us about your third cousin's wife's brother who has work for you. No? Or have you been told you get something for nothing here?

2ND JP.   It's only our own poor who get help from this parish.

1ST JP.   And we don't give money. So you can't drink it. It's your system of poor relief that brings them – they hear there's free bread and cheese, free fuel, there's no parish for miles that does that.

2ND JP.   We can't help every vagrant in the country.

1ST JP.   You must go back to where you were born.

2ND JP.   If her parents didn't come from there they won't take her.

1ST JP.   Her father's parish.

2ND JP.   She's never been there.

1ST JP.   The parish she last lived in.

2ND JP.   They turned her out for begging.

1ST JP.   Exactly, and so do we.

2ND JP.   Why aren't you married?

BROTHERTON. . . .

1ST JP.   Can we please agree on a sentence.

2ND JP.   First offence. Let's be lenient.

1ST JP.   It's only fair to warn you in advance that the next council meeting may reconsider the whole question of poor relief.

2ND JP.   Margaret Brotherton, we find you guilty of vagrancy and sentence you to be stripped to the waist and beaten to the bounds of this parish and returned parish by parish to . . .

1ST JP.   Where she was born.

2ND JP.   To the parish where you were born. Next please.

STAR RECRUITS

      A prayer meeting.

STAR.   Christ watch over this meeting and grant that your kingdom will come, amen.

ALL.   Amen.

STAR.   Life is hard, brothers, and how will it get
          better? I tell you, life in Babylon is hard and
          Babylon must be destroyed. In Babylon you
          are slaves. Babylon is the kingdom of
          Antichrist. The kingdom of popery. The
          kingdom of the king. And it must be
          destroyed. Because then will come the
          kingdom of Jerusalem. And in Jerusalem you
          will be free. That is why you will join as
          soldiers. To destroy Antichrist. To fight with
          parliament for Jerusalem. To fight with
          Christ's saints for Christ's kingdom. Because
          when parliament has defeated Antichrist then
          Christ will come. Christ will come in person,
          God and man, and will rule over England for
          one thousand years. And the saints will reign
          with him. And who are the saints? You are.
          The poor people of this country. When Christ
          came, did he come to the rich? No. He came
          to the poor. He is coming to you again. If you
          prepare for him by defeating Antichrist which
          is the royalists. If you join in the army now
          you will be one of the saints. You will rule
          with Jesus a thousand years. We have just had
          another bad harvest. (BRIGGS *and* FRIEND
          *speak their next speeches – indicated in square
          brackets – at the same time as the rest of* STAR's
          speech from this point on.) But, it is written, when
          Jesus comes 'the floors shall be full of wheat
          and the vats overflow with wine.' Why did
          Jesus Christ purchase the earth with his
          blood? He purchased it for the saints. For
          you. It will all be yours. You are poor now.
          You are despised now. But the gentlemen who
          look down on you will soon find out that the
          inhabitants of Jerusalem are commonwealth
          men. Now is the moment. It will be too late
          when Christ comes to say you want to be
          saved. Some will be cast into the pit, into the
          burning lake, into the unquenchable fire. And
          some will be clothed in white linen and ride
          white horses and rule with King Jesus in
          Jerusalem shining with jasper and chrysolite.

So give now, give what you can to Christ now to pay his soldiers. Christ will pay you back in diamonds. Join now for a soldier of Christ and you will march out of this town to Jersualem. Who are you? What are you? I know you all and you know me. You are nobody here. You have nothing. But the moment you join the army you will have everything. You will be as important as anybody in England. You will be Christ's Saints.

[BRIGGS. Going for a soldier?

FRIEND. What soldier? What side?

BRIGGS. Parliament, inne, Mr Star?

FRIEND. He's a gentleman, inne, Mr Star?

BRIGGS. Parliament's gentlemen. But parliament's for us.

FRIEND. What's the pay?

BRIGGS. More than I'm getting now. And they give you a musket.

FRIEND. For yourself.

BRIGGS. To use it. Heard about the baby.

FRIEND. Ah.

BRIGGS. Wife all right? Thinking of going.

FRIEND. What about . . ?

BRIGGS. Send them money. And where I am now, I'll be out again in the winter like last year. I'm not having that. You keep an eye on them. Won't be long.

FRIEND. Christ's coming anyway.

BRIGGS. You reckon?

FRIEND. Something's going on.]

A LISTENER. And when will Christ come?

STAR. When will Christ come? 'From the abomination that maketh desolate, there shall be one thousand, two hundred and ninety days.' Now a day is taken for a year. And that brings us to sixteen hundred and fifty. Yes, sixteen hundred and fifty. So we haven't much time. Jerusalem in England in sixteen fifty. Don't leave it too late. Join the army today and be sure of your place in Jerusalem.

Now I've a list here of names that have joined already. Twenty-three saints that live in this town. Whose name is next on the list of saints?

BRIGGS.   What's the pay?

STAR.   The pay is eightpence a day. Better than labouring. And it's every day. Not day labour. Not just the days you fight. Every day.

BRIGGS.   And keep?

STAR.   Keep is taken out. But you're given a musket. Shall I take your name?

Three LISTENERS *speak out.*

1ST.   I won't go to fight. But there's three of us could pay for a musket among the three.

2ND.   I've got four silver spoons. They'd pay for something.

3RD.   You can have a buckle I was given.

BRIGGS.   I'll give my name. Briggs. Thomas Briggs.

BROTHERTON MEETS THE MAN

She has several bags. He has a bottle.

BROTHERTON. Went up the road about a mile then I come back. There's a dog not tied up. So I started back where I slept last night. But that was into the wind. So I'm stopping here. It's not my shoes. I've got better shoes for walking in my bag. My sister's shoes that's dead. They wouldn't fit you. How much you got?

MAN.   Drunk it all.

BROTHERTON. I'm not asking.

He gives her the bottle.

MAN. It doesn't matter not eating if you can drink. Doesn't matter not drinking if you can sleep. But you can't sleep in this wind.

He takes the bottle back.

BROTHERTON. What you got there?

MAN. I thought my hands were cold but they're warm to yours.

BROTHERTON. What you got?

MAN. Look, here, that's my Bible. That's my father's name, that's my name. Two and a half acres. I had to sell my knife. I sold my knife.

BROTHERTON. How much you got now then?

MAN. Tenpence.

BROTHERTON. That's a long time till you got nothing. Then you can sell the Bible.

MAN. No, I need that.

BROTHERTON. What I've got, look. The shoes. A bottle, that's a good bottle. I had another one that was no good. I don't often throw something out but I won't carry anything I don't like. A piece of cloth. You can wrap it round. It's got lots of uses. I could sell you that. You can't see what's in here. That's more of my sister's things that's dead. There's a piece of rope. You could have that for a halfpenny.

MAN. Your face is cold. Your neck's cold. Your back's no warmer. The wind goes right through.

BROTHERTON. You can have the rope and the cloth both for a halfpenny.

MAN. Come and lie down. Out of the wind. I'll give you a halfpenny after.

BROTHERTON. No. With tenpence, we can get indoors for that.

MAN.   Wouldn't last long.

BROTHERTON. Last more than one day. Even one day's
               good.

MAN.   If only I knew when Christ was coming.

BROTHERTON. You think he's coming?

MAN.   He must. If only the money would last till the
               world ends then it would be all right. It's
               warm in heaven.

BROTHERTON. If he comes tomorrow and you've not
               drunk your money. Sitting here with tenpence
               in the cold. Christ laugh at you for that.

BRIGGS JOINS UP

               STAR *eats*.

STAR.   You keep your hat on. New style catching on.

BRIGGS.   Yes sir. I mean, yes, I do.

STAR.   As a sign you're as good as me?

BRIGGS.   Yes. Nothing personal, Mr Star. Before God
               only.

STAR.   Parson seen you like that?

BRIGGS.   He said I was a scorpion, sir. Mr Star. I mean,
               he said I was a scorpion.

STAR.   A hat's all right for a soldier. It shows courage.

               Pause, while STAR *eats*.

               You know what I'm eating?

BRIGGS.   Your dinner?

STAR.   What it is.

BRIGGS.   Meat?

STAR.   The name of it.

BRIGGS.   Beef? Mutton? I can't tell from here.

STAR.   Sheep. Or, if it was, cow, but it's sheep. Now
               what language is that, beef, mutton?

BRIGGS.   It's not language –

STAR.   Beef and mutton is Norman words. The Saxon
             raised the animal. Sheep. Cow. The Norman
             ate the meat. Boeuf, mouton. Even the laws of
             this country aren't written in English.

BRIGGS.   So I've come.

STAR.   You haven't got a horse, I know, so I can't put
             you in the horse, though there's more thinking
             men there with hats on and writing their
             grievances down on paper. But you'll find
             plenty to talk about in the foot. Eightpence a
             day and we deduct food and clothing. Cheese
             and hard biscuit. Anything else?

BRIGGS.   You don't know how long it's going to be?

STAR.   Till we win.

BRIGGS.   That's what I mean. How long till we win?

STAR.   What we're fighting for . . . We've known each
             other all our lives. Our paths never cross. But
             you know me as an honest dealer. I've been
             leant on many times to keep up the price of
             corn when it could be down. And I'd be a
             richer man. The hunger now is no fault of
             mine. You're a Saxon. I'm a Saxon. Our
             fathers were conquered six hundred years ago
             by William the Norman. His colonels are our
             lords. His cavalry are our knights. His
             common foot soldiers are our squires. When
             you join this army you are fighting a foreign
             enemy. You are fighting an invasion of your
             own soil. Parliament is Saxon. The Army is
             Saxon. Jesus Christ is Saxon. The Royalists are
             Normans and the Normans are Antichrist. We
             are fighting to be free men and own our own
             land. So we fight as long as it takes. In the
             meantime there's no looting. No raping. No
             driving off of cattle or firing ricks. We're not
             antichristian royalists. We're Christ's saints. It's
             an army that values godliness. There's no
             swearing. The men don't like swearing. They
             like reading their Bibles. They like singing
             hymns. They like talk. We don't discourage

> talk. Your officers are not all gentlemen,
> they're men like you.

BRIGGS. Bacon. Is bacon Norman?

STAR. Pork, Briggs. Pig. Very good.

BRIGGS. And Jacob the younger brother is the Saxon herds the pigs. And Esau the older brother is the Norman eats the pork.

STAR. Very good, Briggs. Excellent. Now one thing. You wear your hat. Will you take orders?

BRIGGS. If they're not against God.

STAR. They can't be against God in God's army.

HOSKINS INTERRUPTS THE PREACHER

PREACHER. My text today is from Psalm one hundred and forty-nine.
'Sing unto the Lord a new song and his praise in the congregation of saints.
Let the high praises of God be in their mouth and a two-edged sword in their hand.
To bind their kings with chains and their nobles with fetters of iron.'

ALL AND HOSKINS. Amen, Amen.

PREACHER. It is no sin to take up arms against the king. It is no sin if we fight singing praises to God, if we fight to bind an unjust king with chains.

ALL. Amen.

PREACHER. For it is written: 'The saints of the most High shall take the kingdom and possess the kingdom forever, even forever and ever.'

HOSKINS. Forever and ever, amen.

ALL. Amen.

PREACHER. The saints will take the kingdom. And who are the saints?

HOSKINS. We all are.

PREACHER. The saints are those whom God has chosen from all eternity to be his people. For he has chosen a certain number of particular men to be his elect. None can be added to them and none can be taken away. And others he has chosen to be eternally damned. As John tells us in Revelation: 'Whosoever was not written in the book of life was cast into the lake of fire.' So it is God's saints, chosen before their birth, written in the book of life, who will bind the king and the nobles and take the kingdom which will last forever.

ALL. Amen.

HOSKINS. But no one is damned. We can all bind the king.

PREACHER. Who are the saints? They are not the same people who rule in this world.

HOSKINS. Amen to that.

ALL. Amen.

PREACHER. When Christ first came to earth he came to the poor. And it is to the poor, to you, to tailors, cobblers, chapmen, ploughmen, that he is coming again. He will not set up a kingdom like we have now, a kingdom of Antichrist, a kingdom of a king, nobles and gentry. In Christ's kingdom no worldly honour counts. A noble can be damned and a beggar saved.

ALL. Amen.

PREACHER. All that counts is whether God has chosen you. Look into your hearts and see whether God has chosen you or –

HOSKINS. He's chosen me. He's chosen everyone.

PREACHER. Or whether you are given over to the devil. For those that are not saved will be cast into the pit. 'And he that cometh out of the midst of the pit shall be taken in the snare.'

HOSKINS. There is no pit, there is no snare.

PREACHER. For now is the time spoken of in Isaiah, 'the earth is utterly broken down, the earth is clean dissolved.'

HOSKINS. God would not send us into the pit. Christ saves us from that.

PREACHER. 'And it shall come to pass in that day, that the Lord shall punish the host of the high ones that are on high, and the kings of the earth upon the earth.'

HOSKINS. Yes he will cast them down but he will not damn them eternally.

PREACHER. Why are you speaking? I let it pass but you are too loud. Women can't speak in church.

HOSKINS. God speaks in me.

PREACHER. For St Paul says, 'I suffer not a woman to teach, nor to usurp authority over the man, but to be in silence.'

HOSKINS. A text? a text is it? do you want a text?

PREACHER. 'For Adam was first formed then Eve. And Adam was not deceived but the woman being deceived was in the transgression.'

HOSKINS. Joel. Chapter two. Verse twenty-eight. 'And it shall come to pass that I will pour out my spirit upon all flesh; and your sons and your daughters shall prophecy, and your old men shall dream dreams and your young men shall see visions. And also upon the servants and upon the handmaids in those days will I pour out my spirit.'

PREACHER. It has got about that I allow answers to my sermons. But this is taking the freedom to speak too far. If anyone can call out whenever they like it will be complete confusion. I allow answers to my sermons if they are sober and godly and if the speaker has the courtesy to wait –

HOSKINS. You say most of us are damned. You say we are chosen to be damned before we are born.

PREACHER. I said to wait till the end of the sermon, and I do not allow women to speak at all since it is forbidden.

HOSKINS. How can God choose us from all eternity to be saved or damned when there's nothing we've done?

PREACHER. I will answer this question because it is a common one and others, who have the grace to wait, may be asking it within themselves. But I am not answering you. How can some people be damned before they are born? Sin is the cause of damnation, but the reason God does not choose to save some people from sin and damnation is his free will and pleasure, not our own.

ALL. Amen.

HOSKINS. God's pleasure? that we burn? what sort of God takes pleasure in pain?

PREACHER. And those few that are saved are saved not by their own virtue though if they are the elect they will by their very nature try to live virtuously, but by God's grace and mercy –

HOSKINS. No, it's not just a few. Not just a few elect go to heaven. He thinks most people are bad. The king things most people are bad. He's against the king but he's saying the same.

PREACHER. Get her out.

Two of the congregation throw HOSKINS *out.*

HOSKINS. In his kingdom of heaven there's going to be a few in bliss and the rest of us in hell. What's the difference from what we've got now? You are all saved. Yes, you are all saved. Not one of you is damned –

PREACHER. Woman, you are certainly damned.

CLAXTON BRINGS HOSKINS HOME

WIFE *is bathing* HOSKINS's *bruised head.*

WIFE. What you go there for?

CLAXTON. When they beat her, you know . . . I
couldn't . . .

WIFE. But who did it?

CLAXTON. They chased her down the hill from the
church and when she fell over . . . I couldn't
stop them. I came up after.

WIFE. But what you go there for?

CLAXTON. Just to see.

WIFE. It's not proper church.

CLAXTON. Just to see.

WIFE. Parson won't like it.

CLAXTON. Parson needn't.

WIFE. I'm not going there if they beat women.

CLAXTON. No but they let you speak.

WIFE. No but they beat her.

CLAXTON. No but men. They let men speak.

WIFE. Did you speak?

CLAXTON. Don't want to work for parson.

WIFE. What then?

CLAXTON. I don't know, I don't know.

WIFE *finishes bathing* HOSKINS's *head.*

HOSKINS. Thank you.

WIFE. Better?

HOSKINS. Yes thank you.

WIFE. Where you from?

HOSKINS. Near Leicester.

WIFE. What are you doing here then?

HOSKINS. Travelling.

WIFE. Are you married? Or are you on your own?

HOSKINS. No, I'm never on my own.

CLAXTON. Who are you with then?

HOSKINS. Different men sometimes. But it's not like you think. Well it is like you think. But then nothing's like you think. Who I'm with is Jesus Christ.

CLAXTON. How do you live?

HOSKINS. Sometimes people give me money. They give me for preaching. I'm not a beggar.

CLAXTON. Didn't say that.

HOSKINS. Steal though if I can. It's only the rich go to hell. Did you know that?

CLAXTON. I think they do.

HOSKINS. And we don't, did you know that?

WIFE. You don't live anywhere?

HOSKINS. I'm not the only one.

WIFE. No one look after you?

HOSKINS. Jesus God.

WIFE. Are your parents living?

HOSKINS. You know how Jesus says forsake your parents. Anyone who hath forsaken houses, or brethren, or sisters, or father, or mother, or wife . . . or children, or lands, for my sake. See.

CLAXTON. No need to go that far.

HOSKINS. Well, it's the times. Christ will be here soon so what's it matter.

CLAXTON. Do you believe that?

HOSKINS. I do.

WIFE. But women can't preach. We bear children in pain, that's why. And they die. For our sin,

Eve's sin. That's why we have pain. We're not clean. We have to obey. The man, whatever he's like. If he beat us that's why. We have blood, we're shameful, our bodies are worse than a man's. All bodies are evil but ours is worst. That's why we can't speak.

HOSKINS. Well I can.

WIFE. You haven't had children.

HOSKINS. That's all wrong what you said. We're not –

WIFE. Have you had a child?

HOSKINS. No but –

WIFE. Then you don't know. We wouldn't be punished if it wasn't for something.

HOSKINS. We're not –

WIFE. And then they die. You don't know.

HOSKINS. They die because how we live. My brothers did. Died of hunger more than fever. My mother kept boiling up the same bones.

WIFE. Go home. Go home.

HOSKINS. No, I'm out with God. You want to get out too.

WIFE. No. No we don't.

CLAXTON. Sometimes I read in Revelation. Because people say now is the last days. 'And I saw a new heaven and a new earth; for the first heaven and the first earth were passed away. And there was no more sea.' Why no more sea? I never seen the sea. But England's got a fine navy and we trade by sea and go to new countries, so why no more sea? Now I think this is why. I can explain this. I see into it. I have something from God. The sea is water. And salt water, not like a stream or a well, you can't drink it. And you can't breathe it. Because it's water. But fish can breathe it. But men can't live in it.

WIFE.   What are you talking about?

CLAXTON.   What it's saying, seems to me. Fish can live in
           it. Men can't. Now men can't live here either.
           How we live is like the sea. We can't breathe.
           Our squire, he's like a fish. Looks like a fish
           too, if you saw him. And parson. Parson can
           breathe. He swims about, waggles his tail.
           Bitter water and he lives in it. Bailiff. Justices.
           Hangman. Lawyer. Mayor. All the gentry.
           Swimming about. We can't live in it. We
           drown. I'm a drowned man.

WIFE.   Stop it, you can't do it, you're making a fool –

HOSKINS.   No, it's good.

CLAXTON.   Octopus is a kind of fish with lots of arms
           grasping and full of black stink. Sharks eat
           you. Whales, you're lost inside them, they're
           so big, they swallow you up and never notice.
           They live in it.

WIFE.   Stop it.

CLAXTON.   We can't live. We are dead. Bitter water. There
           shall be a new heaven. And a new earth. And
           no more sea.

WIFE.   No, don't start. Don't speak. I can't.

COBBE'S VISION

ONE OF THE ACTORS (*announces a pamphlet by Abiezer
           Coppe*). A fiery flying roll: being a word from
           the Lord to all the great ones of the earth,
           whom this may concern: being the last
           warning piece at the dreadful day of
           Judgement. For now the Lord is come to first,
           warn, second, advise and warn, third, charge,
           fourth, judge and sentence the great ones. As
           also most compassionately informing, and
           most lovingly and pathetically advising and
           warning London. And all by his most excellent
           majesty, dwelling in and shining through
           Auxilium Patris, alias Coppe. Imprinted in

London, at the beginning of that notable day, wherein the secrets of all hearts are laid open.

COBBE.   All my strength, my forces, were utterly routed, my house I dwelt in fired, my father and mother forsook me, and the wife of my bosom loathed me, and I was utterly plagued and sunk into nothing, into the bowels of the still Eternity (my mother's womb) out of which I came naked, and whereto I returned again naked. And lying a while there, rapt up in silence, at length (the body's outward form being all this while awake) I heard with my outward ear (to my apprehension) a most terrible thunderclap, and after that a second. And upon the second, which was exceeding terrible, I saw a great body of light like the light of the sun, and red as fire, in the form (as it were) of a drum, whereupon with exceeding trembling and amazement on the flesh, and with joy unspeakable in the spirit, I clapped my hands, and cried out, Amen, Halelujah, Halelujah, Amen. And so lay trembling sweating and smoking (for the space of half an hour). At length with a loud voice I (inwardly) cried out, Lord what wilt thou do with me? My most excellent majesty and eternal glory in me answered and said, fear not. I will take thee up into my everlasting kingdom. But first you must drink a bitter cup, a bitter cup, a bitter cup. Whereupon I was thrown into the belly of hell (and take what you can of it in these expressions, though the matter is beyond expression) I was among all the devils in hell, even in their most hideous crew.

And under all this terror and amazement, a tiny spark of transcendent, unspeakable glory, survived, and sustained itself, triumphing, exulting and exalting itself above all the fiends. And I heard a voice saying, 'Go to London, to London, that great city, and tell them I am coming.'

TWO WOMEN LOOK IN A MIRROR

> 1ST WOMAN *comes in with a broken mirror.* 2ND WOMAN *is mending.*

1ST WOMAN. Look, look, you must come quick.

2ND WOMAN. What you got there?

1ST WOMAN. Look. Who's that? That's you. That's you and me.

2ND WOMAN. Is that me? Where you get it?

1ST WOMAN. Up the house.

2ND WOMAN. What? with him away? It's all locked up.

1ST WOMAN. I went in the front door.

2ND WOMAN. The front door?

1ST WOMAN. Nothing happened to me. You can take things –

2ND WOMAN. That's his things. That's stealing. You'll be killed for that.

1ST WOMAN. No, not any more, it's all ours now, so we won't burn the corn because that's our corn now and we're not going to let the cattle out because they're ours too.

2ND WOMAN. You been in his rooms?

1ST WOMAN. I been upstairs. In the bedrooms.

2ND WOMAN. I been in the kitchen.

1ST WOMAN. I lay on the bed. White linen sheets. Three wool blankets.

2ND WOMAN. Did you take one?

1ST WOMAN. I didn't know what to take, there's so much.

2ND WOMAN. Oh if everyone's taking something I want a blanket. But what when he comes back?

1ST WOMAN. He'll never come back. We're burning his papers, that's the Norman papers that give him his lands. That's like him burnt. There's no one over us. There's pictures of him and

his grandfather and his great great – a long
row of pictures and we pulled them down.

2ND WOMAN. But he won't miss a blanket.

1ST WOMAN. There's an even bigger mirror that we
didn't break. I'll show you where. You see your
whole body at once. You see yourself standing
in that room. They must know what they look
like all the time. And now we do.

BRIGGS RECALLS A BATTLE

BRIGGS.   The noise was very loud, the shouting and the
cannon behind us, and it was dark from the
clouds of smoke blowing over so you couldn't
see more than a few yards, so that when I hit
this boy across the face with my musket I was
suddenly frightened as he went under that he
was on my own side; but another man was on
me and I hit at him and I didn't know who I
was fighting till the smoke cleared and I saw
men I knew and a tree I'd stood under before
the shooting began. But after I was wounded,
lying with my head downhill, watching men
take bodies off the field, I didn't know which
was our side and which was them, but then I
saw it didn't matter because what we were
fighting was not each other but Antichrist and
even the soldiers on the other side would be
made free and be glad when they saw the
paradise we'd won, so that the dead on both
sides died for that, to free us of that darkness
and confusion we'd lived in and bring us all
into the quiet and sunlight. And even when
they moved me the pain was less than the joy.

ALL (*sing from 'Song of the Open Road' by Walt Whitman*).
All seems beautiful to me.
I can repeat over to men and women,
You have done such good to me,
I would do the same to you,
I will recruit for myself and you as I go,

I will scatter myself among men and women as I
   go,
I will toss a new gladness and roughness
   among them.
Whoever denies me it shall not trouble me,
Whoever accepts me he or she shall be
   blessed and shall bless me.

THE PUTNEY DEBATES

RAINBOROUGH. The Putney debates, October the
   twenty-eighth, sixteen forty-seven. I am
   Colonel Thomas Rainborough, a Leveller.

SEXBY.   Edward Sexby, private soldier, elected
   representative or agitator from Fairfax's
   regiment of horse.

RICH.   Colonel Nathaniel Rich.

WILDMAN. John Wildman, civilian, writer of Leveller
   pamphlets who has assisted the agitators in
   drawing up their proposals.

CROMWELL. Oliver Cromwell.

IRETON.   Commissary General Henry Ireton.

CROMWELL. If anyone has anything to say concerning the
   public business, he has liberty to speak.

SEXBY.   Lieutenant General Cromwell, Commissary
   General Ireton, we have been by providence
   put upon strange things, such as the ancientist
   here doth scarce remember. And yet we have
   found little fruit of our endeavours. Truly our
   miseries and our fellow soldiers cry out for
   present help. We, the agents of the common
   soldiers, have drawn up an Agreement of the
   People. We declare:

   First: That the people of England being very
      unequally distributed for the election
      of their deputies in parliament ought
      to be proportioned according to the
      number of inhabitants.

Second: That this present parliament be dissolved.

Third: That the people choose a parliament once in two years.

Fourth: That the power of representatives of this nation is inferior only to theirs who choose them, and the people make the following reservations:

First: That matters of religion are not at all entrusted by us to any human power.

Second: That impressing us to serve in wars is against our freedom.

Third: That no person be at any time questioned for anything said or done in the late wars.

These things we declare to be our native rights and are resolved to maintain them with our utmost possibilities.

CROMWELL. These things you have offered, they are new to us. This is the first time we have had a view of them. Truly this paper does contain very great alterations of the very government of the kingdom. If we could leap out of one condition into another, I suppose there would not be much dispute. But how do we know another company of men shall not put out a paper as plausible as this? And not only another, and another, but many of this kind. And what do you think the consequence of that would be? Would it not be confusion? Would it not be utter confusion? As well as the consequences we must consider the ways and means: whether the people are prepared to go along with it and whether the great difficulties in our way are likely to be overcome. But I shall speak to nothing but that that tends to uniting us in one. And I am confident you do not bring this paper in peremptoriness of mind, but to receive amendments. First there is the question what commitments lie upon us. We have in time of danger issued several declarations; we have

been required by parliament to declare
particularly what we meant, and have done so
in proposals drawn up by Commissary
General Ireton. So before we consider this
paper we must consider how far we are free.

WILDMAN. I was yesterday at a meeting with divers
country gentlemen and soldiers and the
agitators of the regiments and I declared my
agreement with them. They believe that if an
obligation is not just, then it is an act of
honesty not to keep it.

IRETON. If anyone is free to break any obligation he
has entered into, this is a principle that would
take away all government. Men would think
themselves not obliged by any law they
thought not a good law. They would not think
themselves obliged to stand by the authority of
your paper. There are plausible things in the
paper and things very good in it. If we were
free from all other commitments I should
concur with it further than I can.

RAINBOROUGH. Every honest man is bound in duty to
God to decline an obligation when he sees it
to be evil: he is obliged to discharge his duty
to God. There are two other objections: one is
division: I think we are utterly undone if we
divide. Another thing is difficulties. Truly I
think parliament were very indiscreet to
contest with the king if they did not consider
first that they should go through difficulties;
and I think there was no man that entered
into this war that did not engage to go
through difficulties. Truly I think let the
difficulties be round about you, death before
you, the sea behind you, and you are
convinced the thing is just, you are bound in
conscience to carry it on, and I think at the
last day it can never be answered to God that
you did not do it.

CROMWELL. Truly I am very glad that this gentleman is
here. We shall enjoy his company longer than
I thought we should have done –

RAINBOROUGH. If I should not be kicked out.

CROMWELL. – And it shall not be long enough. We are almost all soldiers. All considerations of not fearing difficulties do wonderfully please us. I do not think any man here wants courage to do that which becomes an honest man and an Englishman to do. And I do not think it was offered by anyone that though a commitment were never so unrighteous it ought to be kept. But perhaps we are upon commitments here that we cannot with honesty break.

WILDMAN. There is a principle much spreading and much to my trouble: that though a commitment appear to be unjust, yet a person must sit down and suffer under it. To me this is very dangerous and I see it spreading in the army again. The chief thing in the agreement is to secure the rights and freedoms of the people, which was declared by the army to be absolutely insisted on.

IRETON. I am far from holding that if a man have committed himself to a thing that is evil, that he is bound to perform what he hath promised. But convenants freely made must be kept. Take away that, I do not know what ground there is of anything you call any man's right. I would know what you gentlemen account the right to anything you have in England; anything of estate, land or goods, what right you have to it. If you resort only to the Law of Nature, I have as much right to take hold of anything I desire as you. Therefore when I hear men speak of laying aside all commitments I tremble at the boundless and endless consequences of it.

WILDMAN. You take away the substance of the question. Our sense was that an unjust commitment is rather to be broken than kept.

IRETON. But this leads to the end of all government: if you think something is unjust you are not to obey; and if it tends to your loss it is no doubt unjust and you are to oppose it!

RAINBOROUGH. One word, here is the consideration
now: do we not engage for the parliament and
for the liberties of the people of England?
That which is dear to me is my freedom, it is
that I would enjoy and I will enjoy it if I can.

IRETON.   These gentlemen think their own agreement is
so infallibly just and right, that anyone who
doesn't agree to it is about a thing unlawful.

RICH.   If we do not set upon the work presently we
are undone. Since the agreement is ready to
our hands, I desire that you would read it and
debate it.

IRETON.   I think because it is so much insisted on we
should read the paper.

WILDMAN. Twenty-ninth of October.

IRETON.   Let us hear the first article again.

SEXBY.   That the people of England being very
unequally distributed for the election of their
deputies –

IRETON.   'The people of England.' This makes me think
that the meaning is that every man that is
an inhabitant is to have an equal vote in the
election. But if it only means the people that
had the election before, I have nothing to
say against it. Do those that brought it know
whether they mean all that had a former
right, or those that had no right before are to
come in?

RAINBOROUGH. All inhabitants that have not lost their
birthright should have an equal vote in
elections. For really I think that the poorest he
in England hath a life to live as the greatest
he; therefore truly sir, I think it's clear, that
every man that is to live under a government
ought first by his own consent to put himself
under it.

IRETON.   I think no person hath a right to an interest in
the disposing of the affairs of this kingdom
that hath not a permanent fixed interest in this
kingdom. We talk of birthright. Men may

justly have by their birthright, by their being
born in England, that we should not seclude
them out of England, that we should not
refuse to give them air and place and ground
and the freedom of the highways. That I think
is due to a man by birth. But that by a man's
being born here he shall have a share in that
power that shall dispose of the lands here, I
do not think it sufficient ground.

RAINBOROUGH. Truly sir, I am of the same opinion I
was. I do not find anything in the law of God
that a lord shall choose twenty members, and
a gentleman but two, or a poor man shall
choose none. I find no such thing in the law
of nature or the law of nations. But I do find
that all Englishmen must be subject to English
law, and the foundation of the law lies in the
people. Every man in England ought not to be
exempted from the choice of those who are to
make laws for him to live under, and for him,
for aught I know, to lose his life by.

IRETON.   All the main thing that I speak for is because I
would have an eye to property. Let every man
consider that he do not go that way to take
away all property. Now I wish we may
consider of what right you will claim that all
the people should have a right to elections. Is
it by right of nature? Then I think you must
deny all property too. If you say one man hath
an equal right with another to the choosing of
him that will govern him, by the same right of
nature he hath the same right in any goods he
sees – he hath a freedom to the land, to take
the ground, to till it. I would fain have any
man show me their bounds, where you will end.

RAINBOROUGH. Sir, to say that because a man pleads
that every man hath a voice, that it destroys all
property – this is to forget the law of God.
That there's property, the law of God says it,
else why hath God made that law, Thou shalt
not steal? I am a poor man, therefore I must
be oppressed: if I have no interest in the

kingdom, I must suffer all their laws be they right or wrong. Nay thus: a gentleman lives in a country and hath three or four lordships, as some men have (God knows how they got them); and when a parliament is called he must be a parliament man; and it may be he sees some poor men, they live near this man, he can crush them – I have known an invasion to turn poor men out of doors; and I would know whether rich men do not do this, and keep them under the greatest tyranny that was ever thought of in the world. And I wish you would not make the world believe we are for anarchy.

CROMWELL. Really, sir, this is not right. No man says you have a mind to anarchy, but that the consequence of this rule tends to anarchy. I am confident on 't, we should not be so hot with one another.

RAINBOROUGH. I know that some particular men we debate with believe we are for anarchy.

IRETON. I must clear myself as to that point. I cannot allow myself to lay the least scandal upon anyone. And I don't know why the gentleman should take so much offence. We speak to the paper not to persons. Now the main answer against my objection was that there was a divine law, Thou shalt not steal. But we cannot prove property in a thing by divine law any more than prove we have interest in choosing members for parliament by divine law. Our right of sending members to parliament descends from other things and so does our right to property.

RAINBOROUGH. I would fain know what we have fought for. For our laws and liberties? And this is the old law of England – and that which enslaves the people of England – that they should be bound by laws in which they have no voice! And for my part, I look upon the people of England so, that wherein they have not voices in the choosing of their governors they are not bound to obey them.

IRETON. I did not say we should not have any enlargement at all of those who are to be the electors. But if you admit any man that hath breath and being, it may come to destroy property thus: you may have such men chosen as have no local or permanent interest. Why may not those men vote against all property? Show me what you will stop at.

RICH. There is weight in the objection, for you have five to one in this kingdom that have no permanent interest. Some men have ten, some twenty servants. If the master and servant be equal electors, the majority may by law destroy property. But certainly there may be some other way thought of, that there may be a representative of the poor as well as the rich.

RAINBOROUGH. I think it is a fine gilded pill.

WILDMAN. Our case is that we have been under slavery. That's acknowledged by all. Our very laws were made by our conquerors. We are now engaged for our freedom. The question is: Whether any person can justly be bound by law, who doth not give his consent?

IRETON. Yes, and I will make it clear. If a foreigner will have liberty to dwell here, he may very well be content to submit to the law of the land. If any man will receive protection from this people, he ought to be subject to those laws. If this man do think himself unsatisfied to be subject to this law, he may go into another kingdom.

WILDMAN. The gentleman here said five parts of the nation are now excluded and would then have a voice in elections. At present one part makes hewers of wood and drawers of water of the other five, so the greater part of the nation is enslaved. I do not hear any justification given but that it is the present law of the kingdom.

RAINBOROUGH. What shall become of those men that
have laid themselves out for the parliament in
this present war, that have ruined themselves
by fighting? They are Englishmen. They have
now no voice in elections.

RICH.   All I urged was that I think it worthy
consideration whether they should have an
equal voice. However, I think we have been a
great while upon this point. If we stay but
three days until you satisfy one another the
king will come and decide who will be hanged
first.

SEXBY.   October the thirtieth.

RAINBOROUGH. If we can agree where the liberty of the
people lies, that will do all.

IRETON.   I cannot consent so far. When I see the hand
of God destroying king, and lords, and
commons too, when I see God had done it, I
shall, I hope, comfortably acquiesce in it. But
before that, I cannot give my consent to it
because it is not good. The law of God doth
not give me property, nor the law of nature,
but property is of human constitution. I have
a property and this I shall enjoy.

SEXBY.   I see that though liberty was our end, there is
a degeneration from it. We have ventured our
lives and it was all for this: to recover our
birthrights as Englishmen; and by the
arguments urged there is none. There are
many thousands of us soldiers that have
ventured our lives; we have had little property
in the kingdom, yet we have had a birthright.
But it seems now, except a man hath a fixed
estate in the kingdom, he hath no right in this
kingdom. I wonder we were so much
deceived. If we had not a right to the
kingdom, we were mere mercenary soldiers. I
shall tell you in a word my resolution. I am
resolved to give my birthright to none. If this
thing be denied the poor, that with so much

pressing after they have sought, it will be the
greatest scandal. It was said that if those in low
condition were given their birthright it would
be the destruction of this kingdom. I think the
poor and meaner of this kingdom have been
the means of preservation of this kingdom.
Their lives have not been held dear for
purchasing the good of the kingdom. And now
they demand the birthright for which they
fought. They are as free from anarchy and
confusion as any, and they have the law of
God and the law of their conscience with
them. When men come to understand these
things, they will not lose that which they have
contended for.

IRETON. I am very sorry we are come to this point, that
from reasoning one to another we should
come to express our resolutions. Now let us
consider where our difference lies. We all
agree you should be governed by elected
representatives. But I think we ought to keep
to that constitution which we have now,
because there is so much justice and reason
and prudence in it. And if you merely on
pretence of your birthright pretend that this
constitution shall not stand in your way, it is
the same principle to me, say I, as if for your
better satisfaction you shall take hold of
anything that another man calls his own.

RAINBOROUGH. Sir, I see it is impossible to have liberty
without all property being taken away. If you
will say it, it must be so. But I would fain know
what the soldier hath fought for all this while.

IRETON. I will tell you –

RAINBOROUGH. He hath fought to enslave himself, to
give power to men of riches, men of estates, to
make himself a perpetual slave. We find none
must be pressed for the army that have
property. When these gentlemen fall out
among themselves, they shall press the poor
scrubs to come and kill one another for them.

IRETON.   I will tell you what the soldier of this kingdom
            hath fought for. The danger that we stood in
            was that one man's will must be a law. The
            people have this right, that they should not be
            governed but by the representative of those
            that have the interest of the kingdom. In this
            way liberty may be had and property not be
            destroyed.

RICH.   I hope it is not denied that any wise discreet
            man that hath preserved England is worthy of
            a voice in the government of it. The electorate
            should be amended in that sense and I think
            they will desire no more liberty.

CROMWELL.   I confess I was most dissatisfied with that I
            heard Mr Sexby speak of any man here,
            because it did savour so much of will. But let
            us not spend so much time in debates.
            Everyone here would be willing that the
            representation be made better than it is. If we
            may but resolve on a committee, things may
            be done.

WILDMAN.   I wonder that should be thought wilfulness in
            one man that is reason in another. I have not
            heard anything that doth satisfy me. I am not
            at all against a committee's meeting. But I
            think it is no fault in any man to refuse to sell
            his birthright.

SEXBY.   I am sorry that my zeal to what I apprehend is
            good should be so ill resented. Do you not
            think it were a sad and miserable condition
            that we have fought all this time for nothing?
            All here, both great and small, do think that
            we fought for something. Many of us fought
            for those ends which, we since saw, were not
            those which caused us to venture all in the
            ship with you. It had been good in you to
            have advertised us of it, and I believe you
            would have had fewer under your command
            to have commanded. Concerning my making
            rents and divisions in this way. As an
            individual I could lie down and be trodden

there; but truly I am sent by a regiment, and if I should not speak, guilt shall lie upon me. I shall be loath to make a rent and division, but unless I see this put to a vote, I despair of an issue.

RICH.   I see you have a long dispute. I see both parties at a stand; and if we dispute here, both are lost.

CROMWELL. If you put this paper to the vote without any qualifications it will not pass freely. If we would have no difference when we vote on the paper, it must be put with due qualifications. I have not heard Commissary General Ireton answered, not in a tittle. To bring this paper nearer a general satisfaction and bring us all to an understanding, I move for a committee.

INTERVAL

ACT TWO

DIGGERS

ONE OF THE ACTORS (*announces*). Information of Henry
Sanders, Walton-upon-Thames, April the
sixteenth, sixteen hundred and forty-nine.

One Everard, Gerrard Winstanley, and three
more, all living at Cobham, came to St
George's Hill in Surrey and began to dig, and
sowed the ground with parsnips and carrots
and beans. By Friday last they were increased
in number to twenty or thirty. They invite all
to come in and help them, and promise them
meat, drink and clothes.

WINSTANLEY (*announces*). The true Levellers' standard
advanced, sixteen hundred and forty-nine:

A declaration to the powers of England and
to all the powers of the world, showing the
cause why the common people of England
have begun to dig up, manure and sow corn
upon George Hill in Surrey. Take notice that
England is not a free people till the poor that
have no land have a free allowance to dig and
labour the commons. It is the sword that
brought in property and holds it up, and
everyone upon recovery of the conquest ought
to return into freedom again, or what benefit
have the common people got by the victory
over the king?

All men have stood for freedom; and now
the common enemy has gone you are all like
men in a mist, seeking for freedom, and know
not where it is: and those of the richer sort of
you that see it are afraid to own it. For
freedom is the man that will turn the world

upside down, therefore no wonder he hath enemies.

True freedom lies where a man receives his nourishment and that is in the use of the earth. A man had better have no body than have no food for it. True freedom lies in the true enjoyment of the earth. True religion and undefiled is to let everyone quietly have earth to manure. There can be no universal liberty till this universal community be established.

1ST ACTOR (*announces*). A Bill of Account of the most remarkable sufferings that the Diggers have met with since they began to dig the commons for the poor on George Hill in Surrey.

2ND ACTOR. We were fetched by above a hundred people who took away our spades, and some of them we never had again, and taken to prison at Walton.

3RD ACTOR. The dragonly enemy pulled down a house we had built and cut our spades to pieces.

4TH ACTOR. One of us had his head sore wounded, and a boy beaten. Some of us were beaten by the gentlemen, the sheriff looking on, and afterwards five were taken to White Lion prison and kept there about five weeks.

5TH ACTOR. We had all our corn spoilt, for the enemy was so mad that they tumbled the earth up and down and would suffer no corn to grow.

6TH ACTOR. Next day two soldiers and two or three men sent by the parson pulled down another house and turned an old man and his wife out of doors to lie in the field on a cold night.

1ST ACTOR. It is understood the General gave his consent that the soldiers should come to help beat off the Diggers, and it is true the soldiers came with the gentlemen and caused others to pull down our houses; but I think the soldiers were sorry to see what was done.

CLAXTON EXPLAINS

CLAXTON. Wherever I go I leave men behind surprised I
no longer agree with them. But I can't stop.
Ever since the day I walked over the hill to
Wendover to hear the new preacher for the
first time. And though I'd thought of going for
weeks, the day I went I didn't think at all, I
just put on my coat and started walking. I felt
quite calm, as if nothing was happening, as if
it was an easy thing to do, not something I'd
laid awake over all night, so that I wondered if
it even mattered to me. But as I walked I
found my heart was pounding and my breath
got short going up the hill. My body knew I
was doing something amazing. I knew I was in
the midst of something, I was doing it, not
standing still worrying about it, I was simply
walking over the hill to another preacher. I'd
found everything in my life hard. But now it
seemed everything must be this simple. I felt
alone. I felt certain. I felt myself moving faster
and faster, more and more certainly towards
God. And I am alone, because my wife can't
follow me. I send her money when I can. But
my body is given to other women now for I
have come to see that there is no sin but what
man thinks is sin. So we can't be free from sin
till we can commit it purely, as if it were no
sin. Sometimes I lie or steal to show myself
there is no lie or theft but in the mind, and I
find it all so easy that I am called the Captain
of the Rant, and still my heart pounds and my
mouth is dry and I rush on towards the
infinite nothing that is God.

BRIGGS WRITES A LETTER

STAR.   Writing more letters? Our children grow up
without us. Is there still no news of your wife?
Do you think of leaving the army to look for
her? Because if you don't go to Ireland,
there's not much to do in the army now.

BRIGGS. Enough.

STAR. You make a mistake about Ireland. I understood two years ago, when the men didn't have their back pay, I was with you then. But now it's different. You were agitator of the regiment then and you still –

BRIGGS. I still am agitator of the regiment.

STAR. – Still think you're agitator of the regiment. I know that was a remarkable time for you. To be chosen out of so many. To stand up before the greatest in the country and be heard out. It's a council of officers now, you know that. You know an agitator means nothing. But you won't let it go. You keep on and on. The other men don't admire you for it.

BRIGGS. We're demanding the council be set up like before. You know that. With two agitators from each regiment.

STAR. I know you won't get it. Everyone knows. The other men laugh. You'd far better go home. Or if you still want to serve the cause of the saints, sign for Ireland. Cromwell himself is going, that says something. It's the same war we fought here. We'll be united again. We'll crush the papists just as we did in England. Antichrist will be exterminated.

BRIGGS. But don't you see, the Irish –

STAR. What, Briggs?

BRIGGS. The Irish are fighting the same –

STAR. The Irish are traitors. What?

BRIGGS. Nothing.

STAR. Show me the letter.

BRIGGS. What?

STAR. Show me the letter.

BRIGGS. Can't we even write a letter now without an officer looking it over?

STAR.   It's not to your family.

BRIGGS. No. What then?

STAR.   It's a plot.

BRIGGS. It's a list of proposals.

STAR.   It's mutiny.

BRIGGS. It's a list of proposals. I've made them often
         enough.

STAR.   You have, yes, and nobody reads them now.
         You draw up a third agreement of the people,
         and a fourth, and a tenth. It's a waste of time.

BRIGGS. I waste a few hours then. A few days. If I
         don't get what I fought for, the whole seven
         years has been wasted. What's a few weeks.

STAR.   Show me the letter.

BRIGGS. No.

STAR.   It wasn't an order. You have not refused to
         obey my order. But I won't be able to save
         you from mutiny if that's what you're set on.

BRIGGS. So we can't write now. We can't speak.

STAR.   There's officers above me. Some of them think
         free talk doesn't go with discipline. I've always
         liked talk. I'd be sad to see us lose that
         privilege.

BRIGGS. It's not a privilege. It's a right.

STAR.   If it's a right, Briggs, why was Arnold shot at
         Ware? Why were five troopers cashiered for
         petitioning the council of officers?

BRIGGS. Shall I tell you why?

STAR.   It's not because I knew you before. The whole
         company is my friends. My rank leaves us
         equal before God. And yet my orders have
         been obeyed, because they have been seen for
         what they are, good orders. But lately I am
         talked of by my superiors –

BRIGGS.   Shall I tell you why the Levellers have been shot? Because now the officers have all the power, the army is as great a tyrant as the king was.

STAR.   I can choose to act as if no one is below me. I hope I do. But I can't pretend no one is above me. I have superior officers and I must obey. I don't think you want me removed.

BRIGGS.   You should join us against them.

STAR.   If everyone says and does what he likes, what army is it? What discipline is there? In army or government. There must be some obedience. With consent, I would say, yes, but then you must consent, or – what? If every man is his own commander? There was a time when we all wanted the same. The army was united. I gave orders from God and you all heard the same orders from God in you. We fought as one man. But now we begin to be thousands of separate men.

BRIGGS.   God is not with this army.

STAR.   It is the army of saints.

BRIGGS.   And God's saints shot Robert Lockyer for mutiny. By martial law. In time of peace. For demanding what God demanded we fight for.

STAR.   If the army splits up –

BRIGGS.   It has done.

STAR.   If you Levellers split off into conspiracies away from the main army –

BRIGGS.   It's you who've split off.

STAR.   You risk the King's party getting back again.

BRIGGS.   Would that be worse?

STAR.   Briggs. We can still be a united army. Remember how we marched on London, singing the fall of Babylon?

BRIGGS.   It's you who mutiny. Against God. Against the people.

STAR.	Briggs.
BRIGGS.	It's Cromwell mutinies.
STAR.	Briggs.
BRIGGS.	If I was Irish I'd be your enemy. And I am.
STAR.	Briggs.
BRIGGS.	Sir.

THE WAR IN IRELAND

ONE OF THE ACTORS (*announces*). Soldier's standard to repair to, addressed to the army, April sixteen hundred and forty-nine.

Whatever they may tell you or however they may flatter you, there's danger lies at the bottom of this business for Ireland. Consider to what end you should hazard your lives against the Irish: have you not been fighting in England these seven years for rights and liberties you are yet deluded of? And will you go on to kill, slay and murder men, to make your officers as absolute lords and masters over Ireland as you have made them over England? If you intend not this, it concerns you in the first place to see that evil reformed here. Sending forces into Ireland is for nothing else but to make way by the blood of the army to extending their territories of power and tyranny. For the cause of the Irish natives in seeking their just freedoms, immunities and liberties is exactly the same with our cause here.

THE VICAR WELCOMES THE NEW LANDLORD

VICAR. Mr Star. I wonder if I am the first to welcome you as the new squire.

STAR. And the last I hope. I'm no squire.

VICAR. You've bought the land, that's all I meant.

STAR.   I have bought the land, yes. Parliament is
         selling the confiscated land to parliament men.
         That does not make me the squire. Just as the
         country is better run by parliament than by
         the King, so estates will be better managed by
         parliament men than by royalists. You don't
         agree.

VICAR.   It's not for a parson to say about running an
         estate.

STAR.   No, but you bury the tenants when they
         starve. You'll have fewer to bury. This country
         can grow enough to feed every single person.
         Instead of importing corn we could grow
         enough to export it if all the land was
         efficiently made profitable. The price of corn
         will come down in a few years. Agricultural
         writers recommend growing clover on barren
         land. I will have the common ploughed and
         planted with clover.

VICAR.   An excellent idea.

STAR.   Nettles and thistles cleared, and a great crop.

VICAR.   And the little huts cleared, the squatters' huts.

STAR.   Squatters?

VICAR.   On the common. These last two years.
         Everyone hopes that now the estate is properly
         managed again they will be moved on. They
         are not local people.

STAR.   I haven't been down to the common. Well I'll
         speak to them. All over England waste land is
         being reclaimed. Even the fens. Many years
         ago before the war, Oliver Cromwell himself
         led tenants in protest against enclosing the
         fens. But now he sees, now we all see, that it is
         more important to provide corn for the nation
         than for a few tenants to fish and trap
         waterbirds.

VICAR.   Yes indeed. Yes indeed.

STAR.   When I say enclose the commons, I don't

mean in the old sense, as the old squire did. I
mean to grow corn. To make efficient use of
the land. To bring down the price of corn. I'm
sure the tenants will understand when I
explain it to them.

VICAR.   They will do as they're told. I'm sure you'll
have no trouble collecting the arrears of rent.

STAR.   I know one of the reasons they haven't paid is
because they've had soldiers billetted in every
cottage. So of course I'll give them time to
pay. There is some talk of landlords reducing
rents by as much as the tenants have paid out
on the soldiers.

VICAR.   I have heard talk of that.

STAR.   I hope very much they're not counting on it.
It would make me responsible for the keep for
six years of twenty men and would beggar the
estate.

VICAR.   I told them that. I told them the new squire
wouldn't hear of it.

STAR.   In their own interests. I couldn't afford seed
corn. I need two new ploughs.

VICAR.   I'm sure they know their own interest. They'll
pay.

STAR.   I don't want to evict anyone.

VICAR.   No, indeed, give them time. Three months
would be ample.

STAR.   I thought six.

VICAR.   That's very generous. The tenants will certainly
bless you.

STAR.   I thought I would send for them all to drink
my health and I'll drink theirs.

VICAR.   That is the custom with a new squire. It is
what they expect.

STAR.   Is it? It's what I thought I would do.

VICAR.   Well, I can only say I welcome all the changes

you are making. And I hope you won't make a change so unwelcome to the whole parish as to turn me away after so many years. I know the tenants here are as good and peace-loving as any in England, and I know they'll join me in supporting you in your plans to make this estate prosperous. It's been an unhappy time but the war is over. We are all glad to be at peace and back to normal.

STAR.   It will be hard work. For the tenants and for me. I don't shrink from that. It is to God's glory that this land will make a profit.

VICAR.   I'm sure it will.

STAR.   Don't misunderstand me, Parson. Times have changed.

VICAR.   I'm not against change, Mr Star. So long as there's no harm done.

A WOMAN LEAVES HER BABY

Two women. 1ST WOMAN is carrying a baby.

1ST WOMAN. You'll laugh.

2ND WOMAN. No?

1ST WOMAN. Now I'm here I can't do it.

2nd WOMAN. Waiting for that.

1ST WOMAN. Don't. Don't go. Don't be angry.

2ND WOMAN. We come all this way.

1ST WOMAN. We go back.

2ND WOMAN. Why we bother?

1ST WOMAN. We go back, quick, never mind.

2ND WOMAN. We come so they look after her.

1ST WOMAN. I can't.

2ND WOMAN. I know but just put her down.

1ST WOMAN. Too soon.

2ND WOMAN. Put her down. Just . . .

> *Silence.*

> She die if you keep her.

1ST WOMAN. I can't.

> *Silence.*

2ND WOMAN. What you do then? You got no milk. She not even crying now, see. That's not good. You en had one, I'm telling you, she dying.

> *Silence.*

1ST WOMAN. If I drunk more water. Make more milk.

2ND WOMAN. Not without food. Not how ill you are.

> *Silence.*

1ST WOMAN. What if nobody . . . ?

2ND WOMAN. They will. It's a special house. It's a good town. The mayor himself. Picture inside on the wall with his chain. Mayor himself see her all right.

1ST WOMAN. Another day.

2ND WOMAN. She'll be dead.

1ST WOMAN. If she was bigger.

2ND WOMAN. You're not doing it for you. Do it for her. Wouldn't you die to have her live happy? Won't even put her down. It's for her.

1ST WOMAN. Could die. Can't put her down.

2ND WOMAN. Don't talk. Do it. Do it.

1ST WOMAN. If she was still inside me.

A BUTCHER TALKS TO HIS CUSTOMERS

BUTCHER. Two rabbits, madam, is two shillings, thank you. And sir? A capon? Was yesterday's veal good? Was it? Good. Tender was it? Juicy? Plenty of it? Fill your belly did it? Fill your

belly? It can't have done, can it, or you
wouldn't want a capon today. Nice capon
here, make a fine dinner for half a dozen
people. Giving your friends dinner tonight,
sir? And another night they give you dinner.
You're very generous and Christian to each
other. There's never a night you don't have
dinner. Or do you eat it all yourself, sir? No?
You look as if you do. You don't look hungry.
You don't look as if you need a dinner. You
look less like a man needing a dinner than
anyone I've ever seen. What do you need it
for? No, tell me. To stuff yourself, that's what
for. To make fat. And shit. When it could put
a little good flesh on children's bones. It could
be the food of life. If it goes into you, it's stink
and death. So you can't have it. No, I said you
can't have it, take your money back. You're
not having meat again this week. You had your
meat yesterday. Bacon on Monday. Beef on
Sunday. Mutton chops on Saturday. There's
no more meat for you. Porridge. Bread.
Turnips. No meat for you this week. Not this
year. You've had your lifetime's meat. All of
you. All of you that can buy meat. You've had
your meat. You've had their meat. You've had
their meat that can't buy any meat. You've
stolen their meat. Are you going to give it
back? Are you going to put your hand in your
pocket and give them back the price of their
meat? I said give them back their meat. You
cram yourselves with their children's meat.
You cram yourselves with their dead children.

LOCKYER'S FUNERAL

ONE OF THE ACTORS. From *The Moderate*, a Leveller
    newspaper, April the twenty-ninth, sixteen
    forty-nine.
     Mr Robert Lockyer, a Leveller leader, that
    was shot Friday last was this day brought
    through the heart of the city. The manner of
    his funeral was most remarkable, considering

the person to be in no higher quality than a private trooper. The body was accompanied with many thousand citizens, who seemed much dejected. The trooper's horse was clothed all over with mourning and led by a footman (a funeral honour equal to a chief commander). The corpse was adorned with bundles of rosemary stained in blood, and the sword of the deceased with them. Most of this great number that attended the corpse had sea-green and black ribbons in their hat. By the time the corpse came to the new churchyard, some thousands of the higher sort, that said they would not endanger themselves to be publicly seen marching through the city, were there ready to attend it with the same colours of sea-green and black. Some people derided them with the name of Levellers. Others said that King Charles had not had half so many mourners to attend his corpse when interred, as this trooper.

A few weeks later at Burford, the Levellers were finally crushed.

THE MEETING

A drinking place. The DRUNK *sits apart from the rest.*

HOSKINS (*to* BRIGGS). Come on, plenty to drink. Can't you smile? He wasn't like this last night.

BROTHERTON. What do I do?

COBBE. Anything you like. I worship you, more than the Virgin Mary.

HOSKINS. She was no virgin.

CLAXTON. Christ was a bastard.

HOSKINS. Still is a bastard.

BROTHERTON. I thought you said this was a prayer meeting.

CLAXTON. This is it. This is my one flesh.

COBBE (*to the* DRUNK). Drinking by yourself? Move in with us, come on. Yes, we need you. Get out there when I tell you or I'll break your arm. That was God telling you.

CLAXTON. God's a great bully, I've noticed that. Do this. Do that. Shalt not. Drop you in the burning lake.

HOSKINS. Give us a sip. He won't give us a sip.

CLAXTON. He's not very godly. He needs praying.

HOSKINS. Let us pray. Or whatever.

Silence.

BROTHERTON. When's he coming?

COBBE.   Who?

BROTHERTON. The preacher.

COBBE.   You're the preacher.

BROTHERTON. What? No. I can't.

HOSKINS. Don't frighten her.

CLAXTON. Anyone has anything to say from God, just say it.

Silence.

HOSKINS. There was a preacher. But his head fell off.

Silence.

CLAXTON. It's a fine shining day. Whatever troubles we have, the sky's not touched. A clear day. Let us not lose it. Let us remember the Levellers shot. Those at Burford. Will Thompson and his brother. Private Arnold shot at Ware.

HOSKINS. And the four prisoners in the tower just for writing . . .

BRIGGS.   Avenge Robert Lockyer.

COBBE.   Lockyer's blood. Robert Lockyer's blood. Lockyer's wounds.

BROTHERTON. I don't know these gentlemen. If they

have money. Well if you haven't and you're in the common jail, you're lucky if you don't die. But if they have money for the jailor he gives you a room. With a bed and a window. I was told by a man who'd spent all his money. If you've got money . . .

COBBE.   Damn. Damn. Damn. Damn. Damn.
There's angels swear, angels with flowing hair, you'd think they were men, I've seen them. They say damn the churches, the bloody black clergy with their fat guts, damn their white hands. Damn the hellfire presbyterian hypocrites that call a thief a sinner, rot them in hell's jail. They say Christ's wounds, wounds, wounds, wounds. Stick your fingers in. Christ's arsehole. He had an arsehole. Christ shits on you rich. Christ shits. Shitting pissing spewing puking fucking Jesus Christ. Jesus fucking –

BROTHERTON. Is that from God?

COBBE.   What did you say?

BROTHERTON. Is that from God?

COBBE.   It is, yes. What does he say to you? Does he speak to you? What do you answer? He'll come and speak to you soon enough. The day he comes he'll speak to all of us. He'll come right up to you like this. He wants an answer. What do you say? Nothing? He'll damn and ram you down in the black pit. Is there nothing in you? What are you? Nothing? (To BRIGGS.) Is it nothing but a lifetime of false words, little games, devil's tricks, ways to get by in the world and keep safe? You're plastered over, thick shit mucky lies all over, and what's underneath? Where's your true word? Is there anyone left inside or are you shrivelled away to nothing? (To each.) What will you say? Speak up. What do you answer God? What do you answer? Answer. What do you answer?

HOSKINS. I love you.

COBBE. There. There.

He sits down. BROTHERTON *laughs. Silence.*

CLAXTON. I tell you justice. If every judge was hanged.

HOSKINS. I steal all I can. Rich steal from us. Everything they got's stolen. What's it mean 'Thou shalt not steal'? Not steal stolen goods?

COBBE. Riches is the cause of all wickedness. From the blood of Abel to those last Levellers shot. But God is coming, the mighty Leveller, Christ the chief of Levellers is at the door, and then we'll see levelling. Not sword levelling. Not man levelling. And they feared that. Now God is coming to level the hills and the valleys. Christ break the mountains.

Silence. HOSKINS *holds out an apple.*

HOSKINS. This is something held by a farmer. Then by a stallholder. Then by me. It comes to me God's in it. If a man could be so perfect. Look at it.

She gives it to BRIGGS, *who looks at it, then passes it back to her. She gives it to* BROTHERTON.

BROTHERTON. I always like an apple if I can get it. I haven't been to church for a long time. I don't know if this is a church. It's a drinking place. I always hide on Sunday. They notice you in the street if everyone's in church so I go in the woods on Sunday. I can't see God in this. If God was in it, he'd have us whipped.

CLAXTON. It wouldn't have you whipped, it would bless you. It does bless you. Touch it again. It blesses you. And my hand. Touch my hand. What's the matter?

BROTHERTON. Nobody touches me.

CLAXTON. Why not?

BROTHERTON. They don't touch, I don't know why, nobody touches. I don't count hitting. Nobody's touched me since . . .

CLAXTON. Since what?

BROTHERTON. You don't want to touch me. Don't bother. Pass it on. Pass it on.

HOSKINS. Nobody's touched you since what?

BROTHERTON. It's not right.

CLAXTON. What's not right? Touching or not touching?

BROTHERTON. Both are not right. Pass it on.

CLAXTON. They are, they're both, whichever you want, when you want, is right. Do you want me to touch your hand?

BROTHERTON. No.

CLAXTON. That's right. God's in that too. God's in us. This form that I am is the representative of the whole creation. You are the representative of the whole creation. God's in this apple. He's nowhere else but in the creation. This is where he is.

He gives it to COBBE.

COBBE. I charge at coaches in the street. I shout at the great ones with my hat on. I proclaim the day of the Lord throughout Southwark. And what do they hear? If they could see God in this apple as I do now, God in the bread that they will not give to the poor who cry out day and night, Bread, bread, bread for the Lord's sake, if they could see it they would rush to the prisons, and they would bow to the poor wretches that are their own flesh, and say, 'Your humble servants, we set you free.'

COBBE *gives it to the* DRUNK, *who eats it.*

HOSKINS. There's a man eats God. There's a communion.

BROTHERTON. You don't often see someone eat. They eat when you're not looking.

BRIGGS. Friends. I have nothing from God. I'm sitting here. Nothing. If anyone can speak to my condition.

CLAXTON. You're a soldier?

BRIGGS.   I was.

COBBE.   A Leveller?

BRIGGS.   I was.

CLAXTON. And now?

HOSKINS.   Well, a drink would be best.

CLAXTON. You'll find something. I've been different
         things. When I was first a Seeker, everything
         shone. I thought the third age was coming,
         age of the spirit, age of the lily, everything
         shining, raindrops on the hedges shining in
         the sun, worlds of light. Well, we know how
         parliament betrayed us. Then how the army
         betrayed us. It was all a cheat.

HOSKINS.   Preaching itself is a cheat.

CLAXTON. And then I saw even the Seekers were wrong.
         Because while I was waiting for God, he was
         here already. So God was first in the king.
         Then in parliament. Then in the army. And
         now he has left all government. And shows
         himself naked. In us.

BRIGGS.   We were the army of saints.

CLAXTON. Let it go. Move on. God moves so fast now.

HOSKINS.   I try to be sad with you but I can't. King Jesus
         is coming in clouds of glory in a garment dyed
         red with blood, and the saints in white linen
         riding on white horses. It's for next year. Now
         is just a strange time between Antichrist going
         and Christ coming, so what do you expect in a
         time like this? There's been nothing like it
         before and there never will be again. So what's
         it matter now if we've no work and no food or
         can't get parliament like we want? It's only till
         next year. Then Christ will be here in his body
         like a man and he'll be like a king only you
         can talk to him. And he's a spirit too and
         that's in us and it's getting stronger and
         stronger. And that's why you see men and

women shining now, everything sparkles
because God's not far above us like he used to
be when preachers stood in the way, he's
started some great happening and we're in it
now.

CLAXTON. St Paul to Timothy, 'Let the woman learn in
silence.'

HOSKINS. Jone Hoskins to St Paul, fuck off you silly old
bugger.

They laugh and start getting food out. CLAXTON
holds out food.

CLAXTON. Christ's body.

BROTHERTON. I'm afraid I haven't anything.

CLAXTON. There's plenty.

HOSKINS *holds out wine.*

HOSKINS. This is Christ's blood.

CLAXTON (*to* BROTHERTON). When did you last eat?
Eat slowly now.

BRIGGS. Christ will not come. I don't believe it.
Everything I've learnt these seven years. He
will not come in some bloody red robe and
you all put on white frocks, that will not
happen. All I've learnt, how to get things
done, that wasn't for nothing. I don't believe
this is the last days. England will still be here
in hundreds of years. And people working so
hard they can't grasp how it happens and can't
take hold of their own lives, like us till we had
this chance, and we're losing it now, as we sit
here, every minute. Jesus Christ isn't going to
change it.

CLAXTON. He may not be coming in red.

BRIGGS. He's not coming at all.

CLAXTON. But in us –

BRIGGS. No, not at all.

HOSKINS. He's coming in clouds of glory and the saints –

BRIGGS.   No, no, no.

COBBE.   Do you think God would do all this for
            nothing? Think of the dead. For nothing? Why
            did he call me to warn London? What sort of
            God would he be if he didn't come now?

BRIGGS.   No God at all.

CLAXTON.   But in us. In us. I know there's no heaven or
            hell, not places to go, but in us. I know the
            Bible was written by man and most of it to
            trick us. I know there's no God or devil
            outside what's in creation. But in us. I know
            we can be perfect.

BRIGGS.   Then we must do it.

            COBBE *takes off his coat and throws it at*
            BRIGGS's *feet.*

COBBE.   My coat's yours. And I hope yours is mine.
            We'll all live together, one family, one
            marriage, one flesh in God. That's what we do.

HOSKINS.   Yes, everything in common.

COBBE.   All things common. Or the plague of God will
            consume whatever you have.

CLAXTON.   All goods in common, yes, and our bodies in
            common –

BRIGGS.   No.

HOSKINS.   Yes, we'll have no property in the flesh. My
            wife, that's property. My husband, that's
            property. All men are one flesh and I can lie
            with any man as my husband and that's no sin
            because all men are one man, all my
            husbands one flesh.

COBBE.   I, the Lord, say once more, deliver deliver my
            money which you have to cripples, thieves,
            whores, or I will torment you day and night,
            saith the Lord.

CLAXTON.   We'll take the land, all the land, and Christ
            will come, wait, I have something from God,
            Christ will come in this sense. He will come in

everyone becoming perfect so the landlords all repent stealing the land. Sin is only the dark side of God. So when his light blazes everywhere, their greed will vanish – and that's how evil will go into the pit. Nobody damned, nobody lost, nobody cast out. But Antichrist cast out of us so that we become perfect Christ.

HOSKINS. Perfect men, perfect Christ in the street, I've seen them.

CLAXTON. The rich will be broken out of the hell they are, however they howl to stay there, and when they're out in the light they'll be glad. They'll join us pulling down the hedges.

BRIGGS. The landlords where they were digging at Cobham called the army in. And the soldiers stood by while the diggers' houses were pulled down, their tools destroyed, the corn tramped so it won't grow, men beaten and dragged off to prison. The landlords gave the soldiers ten shillings for drink. Does that sound like the landlords joining us? Does that sound like heaven on earth? I've a friend wounded in Ireland and nearly mad. When they burned the church at Drogheda he heard a man inside crying out, 'God damn me, I burn, I burn.' Is that heaven on earth? Or is it hell?

BROTHERTON. It's hell, life is hell, my life is hell. I can't get out but I'll pull them all in with me.

HOSKINS. No, wait, just wait, you'll see when Christ comes –

BRIGGS. He's never coming, damn him.

COBBE. How we know for certain that God is coming is because of the strange work he has set us on. Who can live through one day the way he used to? I've seen poor men all my life. Last week I met a poor man, the ugliest man I've ever seen, he had two little holes where his nose should be. I said to him, 'Are you poor?' And he said, 'Yes sir, very poor.' I began to

shake and I said to him again, 'Are you poor?'
'Yes, very poor.' And a voice spoke inside me
and said, 'It's a poor wretch, give him
twopence.' But that was the voice of the whore
of Babylon and I would not listen. And again,
'It's a poor wretch, give him sixpence, and
that's enough for a knight to give one poor
man and you a preacher without tithes and
never know when you'll get a penny; think of
your children; true love begins at home.' So I
put my hand in my pocket and took out a
shilling, and said, 'Give me sixpence and
here's a shilling for you.' He said, 'I can't, I
haven't a penny.' And I said, 'I'm sorry to
hear that. I would have given you something if
you could have changed my money.' And he
said, 'God bless you.' So I was riding on when
the voice spoke in me again, so that I rode
back and told him I would leave sixpence for
him in the next town at a house I thought he
might know. But then, suddenly, the plague of
God fell into my pocket and the rust of my
silver rose against me, and I was cast into the
lake of fire and brimstone. And all the money
I had, every penny, I took out of my pocket
and thrust into his hands. I hadn't eaten all
day, I had nine more miles to ride, it was
raining, the horse was lame, I was sure to
need money before the night. And I rode away
full of trembling joy, feeling the sparkles of a
great glory round me. And then God made
me turn my horse's head and I saw the poor
wretch staring after me, and I was made to
take off my hat and bow to him seven times.
And I rode back to him again and said,
'Because I am a king I have done this, but you
need not tell anyone.'

HOSKINS, CLAXTON. Amen.

BRIGGS.   That man will die without his birthright. I've
            done all I can and it's not enough.

CLAXTON. It's not over, there's more, God hasn't
         finished.

BRIGGS. I'll tell you who's with God.

He nods at the DRUNK. HOSKINS *laughs, kisses him, gives him drink.*

BROTHERTON. No I can't. I'm not one of you, I try, you're very kind, I'm not one of you, I'm not one flesh. I'm damned, I know it.

COBBE. You're in hell now but you can come out. Suddenly, suddenly you are out.

BROTHERTON. I mustn't come in a place where God is. It's your fault bringing me here, I'm no good here, I can't be here –

COBBE. We don't want any filthy plaguey holiness. We want base things. And the baseness confounds the false holiness into nothing. And then, only then, you're like a new-born child in the hands of eternity, picked up, put down, not knowing if you're clean or dirty, good or evil.

BROTHERTON. No, I'm wicked, all women are wicked, and I'm –

HOSKINS. It's a man wrote the Bible.

CLAXTON. All damnation is, listen, all it is. Sin is not cast out but cast in, cast deep into God.

BROTHERTON. No I don't want to.

CLAXTON. As cloth is dyed in a vat to a new colour, the sin is changed in God's light into light itself.

BROTHERTON. No.

CLAXTON. That's all damnation is.

BROTHERTON. Let me go.

CLAXTON. It's only God.

BROTHERTON. I must be punished.

HOSKINS. What have you done?

BROTHERTON. Let me go.

COBBE. No, what did you do? God is in me, asking you, God is asking, I am perfect Christ asking

why you damn yourself, why you hold yourself
back from me?

BROTHERTON. Don't touch me. I'm evil.

BRIGGS.   There's nothing you can have done.

CLAXTON. There's no sin except what you think is sin.

HOSKINS. God makes it all, he makes us do it all, he
can't make us sin. The men that crucified
Christ, Christ made them do it.

BROTHERTON. The devil, the devil's got me.

COBBE.   A fart for the devil.

HOSKINS. Don't be frightened. We've got you.

CLAXTON. Sin again, do the same sin as if it were no sin –

HOSKINS. Sin to God's glory.

CLAXTON. Then you'll be free from sin.

COBBE.   You're in heaven, look, you're shining.

BROTHERTON. No, how can I do it again? I did it then
when I did it. It was a sin. I knew it was.
I killed my baby. The same day it was born.
I had a bag. I put it in the ditch. There wasn't
any noise. The bag moved. I never went back
that way.

BRIGGS.   That's not your sin. It's one more of theirs.
Damn them.

COBBE.   God bows to you. God worships you. Who did
he come to earth for? For you. That's
everyone's grief, we take it.

BROTHERTON. He wasn't baptised. He's lost. I lost him.

CLAXTON. Baptism is over.

HOSKINS. No, wait, sit down, listen –

CLAXTON. A baby doesn't need baptism to make him
God, he is God. He's not born evil. He's born
good. He's born God. When he died it was
like a pail of water poured back in the ocean.
He's lost to himself but all the water's God.

COBBE.   Believe us.

HOSKINS.   He's our fellow creature, and you're our fellow
            creature.

CLAXTON.   You're God, you, you're God, no one's more
            God than you if you could know it yourself,
            you're lovely, you're perfect –

BROTHERTON. No, I'm nobody's fellow creature.

HOSKINS.   God now.

COBBE.   Behold, I come quickly, saith the Lord.

CLAXTON.   God's going through everything.

BRIGGS.   Christ, don't waste those seven years we
            fought.

CLAXTON.   Everything's changing. Everything's moving.
            God's going right through everything.

COBBE.   And God for your sin confounds you into
            unspeakable glory, your life, your self.

HOSKINS.   God has you now.

CLAXTON.   Nothing we know will be the same.

BRIGGS.   Christ, help her.

CLAXTON.   We won't know our own faces. We won't know
            the words we speak. New words –

COBBE.   Believe us.

BRIGGS.   Be safe.

HOSKINS.   God has you now.

CLAXTON.   Everything new, everything for the first time,
            everything starting –

BROTHERTON. Yes.

BRIGGS.   Be safe.

BROTHERTON. Yes.

BRIGGS.   So it's over.

BROTHERTON. Yes.

HOSKINS.   There.

BRIGGS.   You can be touched. It's not so terrible. I'll
             tell you what I'll do. Avenge your baby and
             Robert Lockyer. I'll make Cromwell set
             England free. And how? Easy. Kill him.
             Killing's no murder. He wanted to free
             England. That's how he'll do it. Dead.

COBBE.   God won't be stopped.

DRUNK.   I'm God. I'm God.

BRIGGS.   Yes, amen, look who's God now.

DRUNK.   I'm God. And I'm the devil. I'm the serpent.
             I'm in heaven now and I'm in hell.

CLAXTON.   Amen.

COBBE.   You are God. Every poor man.

DRUNK.   I'm in hell, I'm not afraid. I seen worse
             things. If the devil come at me I kick him up
             the arse.

CLAXTON.   And that's the devil gone.

HOSKINS.   Amen, no devil.

DRUNK.   I'm in heaven. And I go up to God. And I say,
             You great tosspot, I'm as good a man as you,
             as good a God as you.

CLAXTON.   And so are we all.

HOSKINS.   And so is everyone in England.

DRUNK.   Plenty of beer in heaven. Angels all drunk.
             Devils drunk. Devils and angels all fornicating.

COBBE.   You are God, I am God, and I love you, God
             loves God.

CLAXTON.   Oh God, let me be God, be clear in me –

HOSKINS.   All the light now –

COBBE.   Sparks of glory under these ashes –

HOSKINS.   Light shining from us –

DRUNK.   And I say to God, get down below on to earth.
             Live in my cottage. Pay my rent. Look after

my children, mind, they're hungry. And don't ever beat my wife or I'll strike you down.

BROTHERTON *gets out some food.*

BROTHERTON. I didn't give you – I kept it back – let me give you –

CLAXTON. Yes, yes, God's here, look, God now –

DRUNK.   And I say to God, Wait here in my house. You can have a drink while you're waiting. But wait. Wait. Wait till I come.

ALL (*sing Ecclesiastes 5, vii–x, xii*).

If thou seest the oppression of the poor, and violent perverting of judgement and justice in a province, marvel not at the matter: for he that is higher than the highest regardeth; and there be higher than they.

Moreover the profit of the earth is for all: the king himself is served by the field.

He that loveth silver shan't be satisfied with silver; nor he that loveth abundance with increase: this is also vanity.

The sleep of the labouring man is sweet, whether he eat little or much; but the abundance of the rich will not suffer him to sleep.

AFTER

HOSKINS. I think what happened was, Jesus Christ did come and nobody noticed. It was time but we somehow missed it. I don't see how.

COBBE.   It was for me, to stop me, they passed the Blasphemy Act. I was never God in the sense they asked me at my trial did I claim to be God. I could have answered no quite truthfully but I threw apples and pears round the council chamber, that seemed a good answer. Dr Higham. I changed my name after the restoration.

BROTHERTON. Stole two loaves yesterday. They caught

another woman. They thought she did it, took her away. Bastards won't catch me.

DRUNK.   The day the king came back there was bread and cheese and beer given free. I went twice. Nobody noticed. Everyone was drunk the day the king came back.

BRIGGS.   I worked all right in a shop for a while. The mercer had been in the army, he put up with me. Then I started giving things away. If a boy stole, I couldn't say anything. So when I left I thought I must do something practical. I decided to bring the price of corn down. A few people eat far too much. So if a few people ate far too little that might balance. Then there would be enough corn and the price would come down. I gave up meat first, then cheese and eggs. I lived on a little porridge and vegetables, then I gave up the porridge and stopped cooking the vegetables. It was easier because I was living out. I ate what I could find but not berries and nuts because so many people want those and I do well with sorrel leaves and dandelion. But grass. It was hard to get my body to take grass. It got very ill. It wouldn't give in to grass. But I forced it on. And now it will. There's many kinds, rye grass, meadow grass, fescue. These two years I've been able to eat grass. Very sweet. People come to watch. They can, I can't stop them. I'm living in a field that belongs to a gentleman that comes sometimes, and sometimes he brings a friend to show. He's not unkind but I don't like to see him. I stand where I am stock still and wait till he's gone.

CLAXTON.   There's an end of outward preaching now. An end of perfection. There may be a time. I went to the Barbados. I sometimes hear from the world that I have forsaken. I see it fraught with tidings of the same clamour, strife and contention that abounded when I left it. I give it the hearing and that's all. My great desire is to see and say nothing.